Alma Flor Ada   F. Isabel Campoy

MERRY NAVIDAD!

Villancicos en español e inglés
Christmas Carols in Spanish and English

illustrated by / ilustrado por Viví Escrivá

English version by / versión en inglés por Rosalma Zubizarreta

Musical consultant / consejera musical: Suni Paz

rayo

An Imprint of HarperCollinsPublishers

Rayo is an imprint of HarperCollins Publishers.

Merry Navidad! Christmas Carols in Spanish and English
Spanish compilation copyright © 2007 by Alma Flor Ada and F. Isabel Campoy
English adaptations copyright © 2007 by Rosalma Zubizarreta
Illustrations copyright © 2007 by Viví Escrivá
Musical notations and adaptations © 2007 by Rosalma Zubizarreta

Manufactured in China.

Library of Congress Cataloging-in-Publication Data
Ada, Alma Flor.
    Merry navidad! : Christmas carols in Spanish and English / Alma Flor Ada ; F. Isabel
Campoy ; illustrated by Viví Escrivá ; English version by Rosalma Zubizarreta = Merry
navidad! : villancicos en español e inglés / Alma Flor Ada ; F. Isabel Campoy ; ilustrado por Viví
Escrivá ; versión en inglés por Rosalma Zubizarreta. — 1st ed.
      p.   cm.
    ISBN-10: 0-06-058434-3 (trade bdg.) — ISBN-13: 978-0-06-058434-4 (trade bdg.)
    ISBN-10: 0-06-058435-1 (lib. bdg.) — ISBN-13: 978-0-06-058435-1 (lib. bdg.)
    1. Villancicos (Poetry) 2. Carols, Spanish—Texts. 3. Folk songs, Spanish—Texts.
4. Children's songs, Spanish—Texts. 5. Folk poetry, Spanish—Translations into English.
I. Campoy, F. Isabel. II. Title.
PQ6209.V5A33 2007   2006028710
398.20946—dc22   CIP
                                                                      AC

Typography by Matt Adamec
1 2 3 4 5 6 7 8 9 10
❖
First Edition

To Collette, Nicholas, Jessica, Cristina, Victoria,
Daniel, Camille, Samantha, and Timothy Zubizarreta—
may you rejoice in knowing the wonder that each of your births
brought to our family
y que siempre florezcan canciones en sus corazones.
—A.F.A.

To Pablo García-Campoy,
the newest and boldest voice in our family chorus,
la más reciente y alegre voz en nuestro coro de familia.
—F.I.C.

For Olmo, Adrián, Paula y Alicia, with all my love—Grandma
—V.E.

Acknowledgments
To Suni Paz, who has turned our poems into songs, for valuable
suggestions and support in the process of creating this collection.
To Tracy Heffernan, for her gentle collaboration in the earlier stages
of this project. To Rosemary Brosnan, who embraces Hispanic
culture with wisdom and enthusiasm.

Índice - Contents

Introducción

La Navidad es una época de celebración para muchos caracterizada por comidas, regalos, decoraciones y . . . ¡música! Quienes hablamos español mantenemos la tradición de cantar villancicos. Algunos villancicos se han venido cantando por siglos.

Los villancicos cruzaron el Atlántico con los colonizadores españoles y viajaron por montañas, desiertos y selvas del Caribe, México y América Central y del Sur. Estos viajes produjeron cambios en ellos, pero su esencia no cambió. Con el tiempo, nacieron nuevos villancicos hispanoamericanos que reflejan los pueblos, los ritmos y las culturas de América Latina. El repertorio de villancicos continúa creciendo.

Hemos seleccionado algunos de los villancicos tradicionales más conocidos en el mundo hispano, así como algunos locales, como Las Posadas, tan importantes en la cultura mexicana y los aguinaldos de Puerto Rico. El libro sigue la trayectoria de los eventos que se celebran del 16 de diciembre al 6 de enero.

El valor de la familia se manifiesta de una manera especial en los villancicos, creando paralelos entre la vida de un hogar latino y de la Sagrada Familia de Belén. Estos versos encantadores, que celebran el milagro de una nueva vida, muestran la fe y la sensibilidad de las culturas hispanas en torno a uno de los temas más importantes de su tradición, la Navidad.

Introduction

The Christmas season is a time of celebration for many people around the world, with special foods, gift giving, decorations, and . . . music! In Spanish, Christmas songs are called *villancicos*, and some of them have been sung for centuries.

Villancicos accompanied the Spanish settlers up the mountains, through the deserts, and into the jungles of the Caribbean, Mexico, and Central and South America. In the course of these travels, some changes were introduced. Eventually new *villancicos* were created, reflecting the people, rhythms, and cultures of the various regions of Latin America. The repertoire of *villancicos* has continued to grow.

We have selected here some of the best-known *villancicos* from the Spanish-speaking world. In addition, we have included others that celebrate regional traditions such as *Las Posadas*, a central feature of Christmas in Mexico, and the Puerto Rican *aguinaldos*. The book is organized chronologically, celebrating events taking place between December 16 and January 6.

Villancicos offer a unique glimpse of the value of family in Hispanic cultures. Their lyrics draw many parallels between the home life of a Latino family and the Holy Family in Bethlehem. These endearing verses celebrate the miracle of a new life and embody the faith and sensibility of Hispanic cultures, as expressed through a central tradition: Christmas, *la Navidad*.

Camino a Belén

El peregrinaje de María y José a la aldea de Belén ha dado origen a muchos villancicos.

Algunos de los villancicos cantan sobre la tristeza de una familia pobre que no encuentra albergue ni apoyo ninguno. Otros cantan sobre la expectativa que se despierta en todos los que al ver pasar a María y José, anticipan el nacimiento del Niño.

El tan popular villancico *Arre, borriquito*, canta sobre el entusiasmo de quienes han recibido el mensaje de la buena nueva y se apresuran para llegar a Belén.

On the Road to Bethlehem

Mary and Joseph's pilgrimage to Bethlehem is commemorated in many *villancicos*.

Some of these songs tell of the sadness of a poor family that is unable to find any shelter or support. Others sing of the excitement that awakens among people as they see Mary and Joseph on their journey and begin looking forward to the birth of the Christ Child.

The very popular *Arre, borriquito* ("Hurry, Little Donkey") sings of the joy of those who have received the good tidings and are rushing toward Bethlehem.

Arre, borriquito

Arre, borriquito,
vamos a Belén,
que mañana es fiesta
y al otro también.

Arre, borriquito,
arre, arre, arre,
anda más de prisa
que mañana es tarde.

Hurry, Little Donkey

Hurry, little donkey,
to Bethlehem with you!
Tomorrow is a feast day
and the next day too!

Hurry, little donkey,
hurry up and *go*!
We need to get there sooner,
before tomorrow!

En un burrito orejón

Villancico andino, de Argentina

No llores más, mi guagüita,
que llega la Navidad.
San José y María vendrán
en un burrito orejón
cargadito de turrón.
San José y María vendrán
y en un burrito orejón
por aquí pasarán.

No llores más, mi guagüita,
que estoy amasando el pan.
Mazapán con miel
y la humita fiel
calentita en la sartén.

Vendrán en un burrito,
caminito para Belén,
por aquí vendrán y te besarán
corazón de mazapán.

On a Long-Eared Donkey

ANDEAN *VILLANCICO*, FROM ARGENTINA

Don't cry, sweet baby, don't cry,
for Christmas is very near.
St. Joseph and Mary will come
on a long-eared donkey,
bringing nougat and fruits,
bringing candy and nuts.

Don't cry, sweet baby, don't cry,
just for you I'm baking bread.
Sweet almonds with honey
and warm tamales
soon, love, you'll be fed.

They will ride here on a donkey
on the road to Bethlehem.
They will come on by
and give you a kiss
sweeter than honey pie.

Hacia Belén va una burra

Hacia Belén va una burra, rin rin,
yo me remendaba, yo me remendé,
yo me eché un remiendo, yo me lo quité
cargada de chocolate.

Cayó frente al molinero, rin rin,
yo me remendaba, yo me remendé,
yo me eché un remiendo, yo me lo quité
su molinillo y su anafre.

María, María, ven acá corriendo,
que los ratoncillos se lo están comiendo.
María, María, ven acá volando,
que los pajarillos se lo están llevando.

A Donkey Goes to Bethlehem

To Bethlehem goes a donkey, rin rin . . .
time to do my sewing, time to sew and mend,
time to rip it out and start it all again,
bearing a load of chocolate . . .

She stumbled in front of the miller, rin rin . . .
time to do my sewing, time to sew and mend,
time to rip it out and start it all again,
dropping the mill and the ground-up cocoa . . .

Oh Mary, dear Mary, please come right away,
for the mice have all started to nibble and play.
Oh Mary, dear Mary, please hurry come quick,
for the birds have all started to flock and to peck.

Las Posadas

La tradición de Las Posadas se originó en México, hacia 1589. En Estados Unidos la celebran no sólo las personas de ascendencia mexicana sino también otros latinos.

Los pobladores indígenas hacían desfiles en el mes de diciembre. Comprendiendo que incorporar las tradiciones locales les ayudaba a propagar la fe católica, los sacerdotes crearon canciones que cuentan la historia de María y José en su camino a Belén en vísperas del 24 de diciembre. Las canciones relatan cómo les negaron albergue hasta que un posadero compasivo les permitió alojarse en el establo donde nació el Niño Jesús.

Las Posadas comienzan el 16 de diciembre y se repiten por ocho noches. La procesión carga imágenes de José y María, aunque a veces dos miembros de la comunidad los representan. El 24 de diciembre la procesión se detiene en la posada donde nacerá el Niño. Esa noche los caminantes traen una imagen del Niño en un pesebre al que festejan cantándole canciones de cuna. Luego celebran con música, baile y una piñata.

Romper una piñata no es tan fácil como parece. Colgada de una cuerda, se puede subir o bajar a voluntad mientras que un niño con los ojos vendados intenta golpearla. Usualmente lo intentan varios niños hasta que la piñata se quiebra y suelta su contenido de dulces y caramelos.

Durante cuatrocientos años muchas canciones típicas han mantenido viva la tradición de Las Posadas. Aquí se incluye una de las muchas que se cantan para romper la piñata.

Las Posadas

The tradition of *Las Posadas* (*posada* means "inn" or "lodging") originated in Mexico, around 1589. It is celebrated in the United States not only by people of Mexican ancestry but by other Latinos as well.

The indigenous people of Mexico traditionally held parades during the month of December. To help propagate the Catholic faith, the priests built on local traditions and created songs about Joseph and Mary walking to Bethlehem. The songs tell how Joseph and Mary were refused shelter until at last a kind innkeeper allowed them to stay in the stable, where the Baby Jesus was born.

Las Posadas begin on December 16 and last for eight evenings. Usually the singers carry images of Mary and Joseph as they walk from house to house, although sometimes two members of the community dress up as Mary and Joseph. On December 24, the procession ends at the *posada* where the Baby Jesus will be born. An image of the Christ Child in a manger is serenaded with lullabies, and people rejoice with music, dance, and a piñata.

Breaking a piñata is not as easy as it seems. The piñata hangs from a rope and can be lifted or lowered while a blindfolded child swings at it with a stick. Usually several children have a turn before the piñata breaks and spills its treasure trove of candies and sweets.

Many traditional songs have helped keep alive the four-hundred-year-old tradition of *Las Posadas*. Here is one of the many songs that can be sung while breaking the piñata.

Para romper la piñata

En las noches de posada,
la piñata es lo mejor.
Los niños más remilgados
se alborotan con fervor.

¡Dale, dale, dale! No pierdas el tino,
mide la distancia que hay en el camino.

Se rompió la piñata,
ahora váyanse yendo;
pero no vayan diciendo:
a mí nada me tocó.

Ahora sí, muchachos, váyanse a dormir,
para que mañana los dejen venir.

Let's Break the Piñata

On the nights of the *Posada*,
the piñata is the best!
Even children who are shy
get as excited as the rest.

Take good aim, take good aim, take good aim and swing!
Keep it up, keep it up, time to try again!

At last the piñata's broken,
now everyone can go home.
We hope no one is complaining,
for the party is over and done.

Yes, now it's really time to head on home and then
rest up for tomorrow, when you will play again.

Nochebuena

El 24 de diciembre o Nochebuena es una noche de celebración para las familias hispanas. La cena de Nochebuena es un momento especial con comidas típicas de cada país o región. Los familiares y amigos a veces recorren largas distancias para celebrar juntos. Suelen traer manjares especiales, como turrones o mazapán, y quizá hasta alguna figura para el nacimiento que muchas familias colocan en un lugar especial de la casa.

Las figuras del nacimiento se van coleccionando a través de los años. Tienen una gran importancia para la familia, no por su valor material, pues muchas son muy sencillas, sino por los recuerdos que atesoran.

En muchos hogares, no sólo hay las figuras básicas que representan a María, José y el Niño, sino también pastores y los Tres Reyes Magos, con camellos cargados de regalos. A veces se crean paisajes con ríos de papel de aluminio y lagunas hechas con espejos, montañas y pueblos que se iluminan en la noche, desiertos de arena con palmeras, cielos repletos de estrellas y trigo sembrado en pequeños recipientes, que se mueven al aire de un ventilador. Es divertido visitar los nacimientos y apreciar la ingeniosidad de sus creadores.

Los villancicos se cantan alrededor del nacimiento y durante varios días, su música inunda la vida familiar y las calles del mundo hispano.

Christmas Eve

Christmas Eve, known as *Nochebuena*, is a night of celebration and joy in the Spanish-speaking world. Families may travel long distances to be together for dinner that night. Every country or region has its traditional foods for the occasion. Visitors may bring some special sweets, such as nougat or marzipan, and perhaps a new figurine for the Nativity scene that many families display in a prominent place in their home.

The Nativity figurines are often collected over the course of many years. They are treasured by families, not primarily for their material value, as the figurines can be very simple, but instead for the memories they hold.

In addition to the basic figurines representing Mary, Joseph, and the Baby Jesus, many Nativity scenes also include the shepherds and the Three Wise Men with camels bearing presents. Some families create an entire landscape, with towns that can be lit up at night, rivers made of aluminum foil, mountains of papier-mâché, ponds and lakes made with small mirrors, and green fields made with trays of sprouted wheat. Friends and neighbors often drop by to admire these special Nativity scenes and appreciate the ingenuity of their creators.

Villancicos are often sung around the Nativity. For several days their special music permeates both family life at home as well as outdoor street celebrations throughout the Hispanic world.

Campana sobre campana

Campana sobre campana
y sobre campanas una,
asómate a la ventana
verás al Niño en la cuna.

Belén, campanas de Belén,
que los ángeles tocan
¿qué nueva nos traéis?

—Recogido tu rebaño
¿a dónde vas, pastorcito?
—Voy a llevar al portal
requesón, manteca y vino.

Belén, campanas de Belén,
que los ángeles tocan
¿qué nueva nos traéis?

Bells Upon Bells

Bells upon bells have been ringing,
bells have been ringing all day long.
Come to the window and see
the newly born Child in his cradle.

Oh, bells, the bells of Bethlehem,
sweet music of the angels,
what good news do you bring?

As your sheep are now all gathered,
where shall you go to, oh shepherd?
"To the manger with a gift,
cheese and butter from my milkherd."

Oh, bells, the bells of Bethlehem,
sweet music of the angels,
what good news do you bring?

Resuenen con alegría

JOTA ESPAÑOLA,
ACOMPAÑADA POR CASTAÑUELAS

Resuenen con alegría

los cánticos de mi tierra

que viva el Niño Jesús

que ha nacido en Nochebuena.

La Nochebuena se viene

tu-ru-ru

la Nochebuena se va

y nosotros nos iremos

tu-ru-ru

y no volveremos más.

24

It's Time to Sing Out with Joy

JOTA (A FOLK DANCE) FROM SPAIN,
TO BE PLAYED WITH CASTANETS

It's time to sing out with joy

the songs that are sung in my land

in praise of the precious Child

born this holy Christmas evening.

The eve of Christmas is coming,

tu ru ru,

the eve of Christmas is past

and soon we will all be leaving,

tu ru ru,

and we won't be coming back.

¡Fum, fum, fum!

En Belén están de fiesta,
¡fum, fum, fum!
El motivo del contento
no adivino, ¿cuál será?
Y con tanta alegría
les va a sorprender el día,
¡fum, fum, fum!

Hoy Belén está de fiesta,
¡fum, fum, fum!
Porque vienen los pastores
presurosos a anunciar
con muchísima alegría
que ha nacido el Mesías,
¡fum, fum, fum!

Al compás de los panderos,
¡fum, fum, fum!
se está despertando el mundo
lleno de felicidad,
porque no hay mayor consuelo
que adorar al Rey del Cielo,
¡fum, fum, fum!

Al compás de los panderos,
¡fum, fum, fum!
la feliz Virgen María
va meciendo al Niño Dios,
y a pesar de tales truenos
muy tranquilo está durmiendo,
¡fum, fum, fum!

Desde el cielo está mirando,
¡fum, fum, fum!
a la tierra rutilante
que deslumbra con su luz
en la paz del firmamento
celebrando el nacimiento
de Jesús.

Fum, Fum, Fum!

Bethlehem is celebrating,
fum, fum, fum!
What's the reason for such glee?
What can it be? I cannot guess.
So much joy that fills the day,
a wondrous gift is here to stay!
Fum, fum, fum!

Bethlehem is celebrating,
fum, fum, fum!
All the shepherds make great haste,
they have such news they want to tell,
that our new Redeemer's born
on this radiant Christmas morn,
fum, fum, fum!

28

To the sound of tambourines,
fum, fum, fum!
All the world's awakening to a new day
that's filled with joy
Christ has come to be our King,
now our hearts are free to sing,
fum, fum, fum!

To the music of the drums,
fum, fum, fum!
The Virgin Mary rocks the cradle,
as the Baby falls asleep,
Never mind the music's thunder,
He lies still in a sweet slumber,
fum, fum, fum!

From the skies the angels watch,
fum, fum, fum!
A glowing earth that shines so bright
and fills the heavens with her light,
peace and joy are here on earth,
as we celebrate the birth
of the Christ!

Los pastores

En la tradición de los villancicos, los pastores representan a la gente humilde que el Niño Jesús viene a proteger. La generosidad de los pastores se manifiesta en muchos de los villancicos, donde le traen al Niño los modestos regalos que le pueden ofrecer: frutas, queso, flores. Ningún regalo es demasiado humilde porque no es el valor material el que cuenta sino la generosidad y el amor con que se ofrece.

El tema del regalo de los pastores aparece también en la obra navideña tradicional *La pastorela* que el Teatro Campesino presenta cada año en San Juan Bautista, California.

En los villancicos, los pastores representan también el aspecto humano y gozoso de la Navidad. Se dirigen al recién nacido en una forma familiar, con risas, alegría e incluso bromas.

The Shepherds

In the tradition that the *villancicos* celebrate, the shepherds represent the humble people whom the Baby Jesus has come to help. The shepherds' generosity is shown by the simple gifts they bring the Child: fruits, cheese, flowers. No offering is too humble, as the gifts are measured not by their material value but by the generosity and love with which they are given.

The gift of the shepherds is also the theme of a traditional Hispanic Christmas play, *La pastorela* (*The Shepherds' Song*), which is enacted every year in San Juan Bautista, California, by the Teatro Campesino (The Farm Workers' Theater).

In the *villancicos*, the shepherds also embody the playful and human side of Christmas. They tend to address the newborn Child in an informal and intimate manner, often with joy and laughter and at times even with gentle teasing.

Al Niño bonito

DE TUCUMÁN, ARGENTINA

Al Niño bonito
¿qué le daré?
Un conejito
que ayer pillé.
Es muy mansito,
no sabe morder.
Aquí se lo traigo
para que juegue
con Su Merced.

To the Beautiful Child

FROM TUCUMÁN, ARGENTINA

What gift shall I bring thee,

beautiful Child?

Here is a bunny

who is not too wild.

Bunny's very tame,

he will never bite.

I bring him as a gift

so that he can play

with Thee, Child of Light.

Pastores, venid

Pastores, venid,
pastores, llegad,
a adorar al Niño,
a adorar al Niño,
que ha nacido ya.

Todos los pastores
saltan de alegría,
porque ya nació
porque ya nació
el hijo de María.

Yo traeré gustoso
como pastorcito
un par de pichones
un par de pichones
con un corderito.

Come, Shepherds, Come

Come, shepherds, come,
come, shepherds, come,
to adore the Christ Child,
to adore the Christ Child,
who has just been born.

Every single shepherd
is jumping with joy
at the Baby's birth,
at the Baby's birth,
Mary's darling boy.

As a little shepherd,
joyfully I'll bring,
a pair of newborn doves,
a pair of newborn doves
and a baby lamb.

Nanas de Navidad

Algunos villancicos son arrullos, canciones de cuna para dormir al Niño. María le canta al Niño como lo haría cualquier madre con su pequeñuelo, alabando su belleza, diciéndole como el mundo entero quiere velar su sueño.

Algunas de estas nanas le cantan a toda la familia. Invitan al Niño a reír porque ya le cambiaron los pañales. Reconocen que María ha lavado mucha ropa en el río y que José es un buen carpintero que sabe hacer una cuna para el recién nacido. Y la abuela Santa Ana aparece como la que le da regalos al Niño.

Estas nanas de Navidad han trascendido su origen: las madres las cantan en cualquier época del año para dormir a sus niños.

Christmas Lullabies

Some *villancicos* are lullabies, songs to soothe the Child and help him sleep. Mary sings to her Child as any mother would, admiring his beauty and letting him know that the entire world watches over him as he sleeps.

Some *villancicos* sing to the whole family. The lyrics invite the Child to laugh, now that his mother has changed his diapers. They also acknowledge all of the laundry that Mary has been washing in the river, and praise Joseph's skill at making a cradle for his newborn. Baby Jesus' grandmother, Saint Ann, sometimes appears bringing treats.

Many of these Christmas lullabies have transcended their origins and are often sung by mothers to their own infants at any time of year.

A la nanita, nana

A la nanita nana, nanita nana,
nanita ea,
mi Jesús tiene sueño,
bendito sea, bendito sea.

Fuentecilla que corre,
clara y sonora,
ruiseñor que en la selva
cantando llora:
callad mientras la cuna
se balancea.

A la nana nanita, nanita nana, nanita ea . . .

Hush-a-bye, Sweet Baby

Hush-a-bye, sweet Baby, hush-a-bye, dear Child,
hush-a-bye Baby,
my dear Jesus is sleepy,
oh blessed be, oh blessed be.

Tiny fountain that sparkles
and babbles as it flows,
nightingale that calls out
such sad and lovely songs,
hush now, please be quiet
while the cradle rocks.

Hush-a-bye, sweet Baby, hush-a-bye, dear Child . . .

Los peces en el río

La Virgen se fue a lavar
sus manos blancas al río:
el sol se quedó parado,
la mar perdió su ruido.

Ay, pero mira cómo beben los peces en el río,
pero mira cómo beben por ver a Dios nacido.
Beben y beben y vuelven a beber
los peces en el río por ver a Dios nacer.

La Virgen está lavando
y tendiendo en el romero,
los pajaritos cantaban
y el agua se iba riendo. [*Ay, pero mira . . .*]

La Virgen quiso sentarse
al abrigo de un olivo;
y las hojas se volvieron
a ver al recién nacido. [*Ay, pero mira . . .*]

The Fish in the River

Sweet Mary went down to wash
her tender hands in the river;
the Sun stood still in the sky,
the Ocean a silent shiver.

Oh, what a sight to see the fish, they're drinking in the river,
oh, see them celebrating that Jesus Christ is born.
Drinking and drinking and drinking yet once more . . .
oh, see them celebrating that Jesus Christ is born.

Sweet Mary's washing the diapers
and spreading them out to dry.
Birds sing and the waters laugh
as the river flows on by. . . . [*Oh, what a sight . . .*]

Sweet Mary sat down to rest
'neath the shade of an olive tree.
Each silvery leaf did turn 'round,
the newborn Baby to see. [*Oh, what a sight . . .*]

Arrurrú

Villancico tradicional, de Chile

Señora doña María,
aquí le traigo a mi hijito
para que le mueva la cuna
cuando llore su niñito.

Arrurrú, arrurrú,
duérmete Niño Jesús.

Juan Manuel se llamará
de apellido Echeverría.
Para cuando usted lo llame
señora, doña María. [*Arrurrú . . .*]

Señora doña María,
deje acercarme un poquito
y sin despertar al niño
besarle los piececitos. [*Arrurrú . . .*]

Arrurrú, Rock-a-Bye

TRADITIONAL *VILLANCICO*, FROM CHILE

My lady, doña María,
I'm bringing my child to you
so he can help rock the cradle
when your little Baby cries.

Arrurú, rock-a-bye,
go to sleep, my dear Christ Child.

I've named him Juan Manuel;
his last name is Echeverría;
call him whenever you need him,
my lady, doña María. [*Arrurrú . . .*]

My lady, doña María,
I would like a closer peek.
I'll try not to wake the Baby
while I kiss his little feet. [*Arrurrú . . .*]

43

San José

San José es una figura amada en el mundo hispano, donde muchos niños llevan su nombre. Los villancicos lo celebran como un hombre gentil y cariñoso que cuida de María y del Niño. Pero San José es también el protagonista de graciosas y alegres rimas. Algunos villancicos cuentan cómo las barbas de José le hacen cosquillas al Bebé, o cómo los ratones le han comido los pantalones.

Esta familiaridad muestra a la Sagrada Familia como modelo de una familia humana cercana y cariñosa.

Saint Joseph

Saint Joseph is a beloved figure in the Hispanic world; many boys are named José in his honor. In *villancicos*, Saint Joseph is celebrated as a gentle, kind man who takes care of Mary and the Christ Child. But Saint Joseph is also the subject of delightful rhymes filled with fun and laughter. Some *villancicos* sing of how Joseph's beard tickles the newborn Child, or how the mice have eaten Saint Joseph's trousers.

This kind of familiarity is often found in *villancicos* and serves to portray the Holy Family as a warm and accessible human family.

Este niño tiene sueño

Este niño tiene sueño
no tiene cama ni cuna;
San José, que es carpintero,
le diré que le haga una.

This Child Is Sleepy

This Child is tired and sleepy,
yet he has no crib nor bed.
Saint Joseph, you're a carpenter;
please make something to rest his head.

45

El árbol de Navidad

En algunos países hispanos se acostumbra alumbrar las calles con guirnaldas de bombillos de colores de variadas formas. También se usan banderines de papel de seda recortados con gran arte.

Las luminarias son sacos de papel llenos de arena con una velita dentro. Se las ve iluminando las veredas o en los techos de las casas en Nuevo México, Arizona y algunas zonas de Texas.

En el mundo hispano es frecuente ver nacimientos en las iglesias, en lugares públicos y en los hogares. Algunos de ellos pueden ser muy elaborados. Muchas personas acompañan el nacimiento con un arbolito de Navidad. Los siguientes villancicos le rinden homenaje al árbol de Navidad.

The Christmas Tree

In some Spanish-speaking countries, it is traditional to decorate the streets with strings of multicolored lights forming different designs. Paper banners with intricate cutout patterns are another traditional decoration.

Luminarias are paper bags filled with sand that hold a small candle inside. They can be seen in New Mexico, Arizona, and certain areas of Texas, lighting up the sidewalks or rooftops at night.

Throughout the Spanish-speaking world, one often finds Nativity scenes in churches, public places, and homes. Some Nativity scenes can be very elaborate. Many people accompany their Nativity scene with a Christmas tree. The following *villancicos* serenade the Christmas tree.

La hojita del pino

La hojita del pino
tan alta que está
siendo menudita
¿quién la cogerá?

Responde la Virgen:
—Yo la cogeré
la hojita del pino
para San José.

The Pine Tree Needle

See the pine tree needle
so high overhead . . .
such a tiny needle,
who will gather it?

The Virgin Mary answers,
"I will gather it,
the tiny pine tree needle
for my dear St. Joseph."

Arbolito

Esta noche es Nochebuena,
vamos al bosque, hermanito,
a cortar un arbolito
porque la noche es serena.

Los Reyes y los pastores
andan siguiendo una estrella
le cantan al Niño Jesús
hijo de la Virgen bella.

Arbolito, arbolito,
campanitas te pondré
quiero que seas bonito
que al recién nacido
te voy a ofrecer.

Iremos por el camino
caminito de Belén
iremos porque esta noche
ha nacido el Niño Rey.

Christmas Tree

On this quiet Christmas evening,
let's head out into the forest,
to find a young tree to bring home.
Come with me, my little brother!

The Three Wise Men and the shepherds
journey to follow a bright star.
They sing to the Baby Jesus,
son of our dear Virgin Mary.

Christmas tree, oh, Christmas tree,
I'll fill your branches with bright bells.
I want you to look so lovely
as you'll be my gift to
the sweet newborn Babe.

We'll set forth out on the road,
on the road to Bethlehem. . . .
We'll set forth because tonight
the Christ Child has come to reign.

Aguinaldos

La costumbre de los aguinaldos se remonta a la época medieval. El día después de Navidad, y en conmemoración del nacimiento de Jesús, era costumbre repartir limosnas a los pobres en las iglesias y conventos.

La tradición fue ampliándose para dar pequeños obsequios, muchas veces de dinero, llamados "aguinaldos" a las personas que a lo largo del año ofrecen un servicio.

En Puerto Rico, la palabra aguinaldo pasó a ser además el nombre de un tipo especial de villancico en el que se pide que abran la puerta e inviten a comer y beber a quien ha llegado.

Aguinaldos

The tradition of *aguinaldos* goes back to the Middle Ages. The day after Christmas, to commemorate the birth of Jesus, it was customary for churches and convents to offer alms to the poor.

The tradition grew over the years to include the custom of giving small gifts, or *aguinaldos*, often in the form of money, to people who performed a service throughout the course of the year.

In Puerto Rico, the word *aguinaldo* also became the name given to a special kind of *villancico*, in which the singer knocks at the door and asks to be invited in for dinner or a treat.

Ábranme la puerta

Ábranme la puerta
que yo quiero entrar
que hechos mis pasteles
no pueden quedar.

Ah, las arandelas de mi corazón.

Oiga, usted, María,
la quiero y la adoro,
pero mi aguinaldo
no se lo perdono.

Open Wide the Door

Open wide the door;
I'd like to come on in!
I've baked some treats to share,
so let the feast begin.

*Oh, the ties that bind us
to a loving heart. . . .*

Listen, dearest Mary,
I worship and adore you,
but my Christmas favors
I will not forgo.

De las montañas venimos

TRADICIONAL, DE PUERTO RICO

De las montañas venimos
para invitarlo a comer
un lechoncito en su vara
y ron pitorro a beber.

Ay, doña María, ay, compay José,
ábranme la puerta que los quiero ver.

Ábrame, comadre,
que ya son las tres
y yo no he probado
gota de café.

Sin arroz con dulce
pasteles y ron
estas Navidades
no las paso yo.

54

We Come Down from the Mountains

TRADITIONAL, FROM PUERTO RICO

We come down from the mountains
to invite you to dine
on a suckling pig we've roasted
and homemade rum for wine.

Ay, doña María, ay, compay José,
I'm knocking at your door,
here to see you today.

Open up, my friend,
for it's already three
and I still have not yet had
a single drop of tea.

Without my rice pudding,
pastries, and warm rum,
this long-awaited Christmas
will be short on fun.

Los tres Reyes Magos

Según la tradición, los tres Reyes Magos le trajeron regalos al Niño Jesús el 6 de enero. En muchos de los países de habla hispana, ése es el día en que se intercambian regalos y los niños se despiertan para encontrarse con la generosidad de los reyes. En algunos países se comparten golosinas especiales, ya que éste es el día en que acaban las festividades de las Navidades. La rosca de Reyes es una rosca de pan dulce que lleva pequeños regalos adentro. Se dice que quien los encuentra tendrá un año próspero.

A los Reyes Magos, Melchor, Gaspar y Baltasar, se los representa de distinta manera. Generalmente uno es viejo, con barba blanca, y viene de Persia. Otro es africano, con piel y ojos oscuros. Y el tercero viene de Arabia. Algunas veces los tres aparecen montados en camellos; otras veces, montan a caballo, pero siempre traen camellos cargados de regalos. También se los ve montando otros animales, como caballos blancos o elefantes.

Los Reyes Magos despiertan la imaginación de los niños y adultos. A veces, en la noche del 5 de enero, los niños dejan junto a los zapatos agua y hierba para los camellos, caballos y elefantes que deben tener mucha sed después de haber atravesado el desierto.

¡Qué alegría cuando a la mañana siguiente el agua y la hierba han desaparecido y los zapatos están llenos de regalos!

The Three Wise Kings

According to tradition, the Three Wise Kings brought presents to the Christ Child on the sixth day of January. In many Spanish-speaking countries, that is the day on which presents are exchanged and children wake up to find the surprises that the generous kings have brought them. In some countries, special sweets are shared on this day, as it marks the end of the Christmas celebrations. The *rosca de Reyes* is a loaf of sweet bread that hides little presents inside. Those who find the gifts are said to have a prosperous year ahead.

The three *Reyes Magos*—Melchior, Caspar, and Balthasar—are pictured in diverse ways. Usually one is an older man with a white beard, of Persian origin. Another is African, with dark skin and eyes. The third is Arabian. Sometimes all three kings are shown riding on camels; other times they are shown on horseback, leading camels loaded with gifts. Occasionally they each ride a different animal: the first king rides a white horse, the second an elephant, and the third a camel.

The *Reyes Magos* inspire the imagination of young and old alike. On the night of January fifth, children often set out water and grass next to their shoes for the camels, horses, and elephants, who must be quite thirsty and hungry after having crossed the desert.

The next morning is a joyful celebration, as children awaken to find the water and grass gone, and their shoes now filled with gifts!

Ya vienen los Reyes

Ya vienen los Reyes
por los arenales
ya le traen al Niño
muy ricos pañales.

Manzanita verde
hojas de limón
la Virgen María
madre del Señor.

The Three Wise Kings Are Coming

The Three Wise Kings are coming
across the sandy deserts.
Among the gifts they're bringing
are the softest diapers.

Oh, little green apples
and lemon tree leaves,
the sweet Virgin Mary
gives Baby a kiss.

El cielo de Belén

El cielo de Belén
ya se pone claro
que asoma la estrella
de los Reyes Magos.

The Sky in Bethlehem

The sky in Bethlehem
is shining, oh, so bright,
now that the Wise Kings' star
has come to share her light.

Hacia Belén va una burra

Campana sobre campana

Cam - pa - na so - bre cam - pa - na, y so - bre cam - pa - nas u - na,
Bells u - pon bells have been ring - ing, bells have been ring - ing all day long,

á - so - ma - te a la ven - ta - na, ve - rás al Ni - ño en la
come to the win - dow and see _____ the new - ly born Child in his

cu - na. Be - lén, cam - pa - nas de Be - lén, que los án - ge - les
cra - dle. Oh bells, the bells of Beth - le - hem, sweet mu - sic of the

to _ - can, ¿qué nue - va nos tra - éis? Re - co - gi - do tu re - ba _ - ño,
an - gels, what good news do you bring? As your sheep are now all ga _ - thered,

¿a dón - de vas pas - tor - ci _ - to? Voy a lle _ - var al por tal _____
where shall you go to, o shep _ - herd? To the man _ - ger with a gift _____

re - que - són, man - te - ca y vi _ - no. Be - lén, cam - pa - nas de Be -
cheese and but - ter from my milk _ - herd. Oh bells, the bells of Beth - le -

lén, que los án - ge - les to _ - can, ¿qué nue - va nos tra - éis?
hem, sweet mu - sic of the an - gels, what good news do you bring?

¡Fum, fum, fum!

En Be - lén es - tán de fies - ta, ¡fum, fum, fum! En Be - lén es -
Beth - le - hem is ce - le - bra - ting, fum, fum, fum! Beth - le - hem is

tán de fies - ta, ¡fum, fum, fum! El mo - ti - vo del con -
ce - le - bra - ting, fum, fum, fum! What's the rea - son for such

ten - to no a - di - vi - no, ¿cuál se - rá? Y con tan - ta a - le -
glee? What can it be? I can - not guess! So much joy that fills the

grí - a les va a sor - pren - der el dí - a, ¡fum, fum, fum!
day, a won - drous gift is here to stay___ fum, fum, fum!

A la nanita nana

A la na - ni - ta na - na, na - ni - ta na - na, na - ni - ta e - a, mi Je - sús tie - ne
Hush - a - bye sweet Ba - by, hush - a - bye dear Child, hush - a - bye___ Ba - by, my dear Je - sus is

sue - ño, ben - di - to se - a, ben - di - to se - a. Fuen - te - ci - lla que co - rre,
sleepy, oh___ bless - ed be, oh___ bless - ed be___. Ti - ny foun - tain that spark - les,

cla - ra y so - no - ra, rui - se - ñor que en la sel - va, can - tan - do llo - ra,
and bab - bles as it flows, night - ing - gale that___ calls out, such sad and love - ly songs,

ca - llad mien - tras la cu - na, se ba - lan - ce - a. A la na - ni - ta na - na, na - ni - ta e __ a.
hush now please be qui - - et, while the cra - dle rocks. Hush - a - bye sweet Ba __ - by, hush - a - bye dear Child.

Los peces en el río

La Vir-gen se fue a la -var,_____ sus ma-nos blan-cas al rí_____
Sweet Ma-ry went down to wash, _____ her ten-der hands in the ri_____

o, el sol se que-dó pa-ra _____ do, la mar per-dió su rui_____
ver, the Sun stood still in the sky,_____ the O-cean a si-lent shi_____

do. Ay, pe-ro mi-ra có-mo be-ben, los pe-ces en el rí-o, pe-ro
ver. Oh, what a sight to see the fish __, they're drin-king in the ri-ver, oh__

mi-ra có-mo be-ben, por ver a Dios na-ci-do. Be-ben y be-ben y
see them ce-le-bra-ting, that Je-sus Christ is born. Drink-ing and drink-ing and

vuel-ven a be-ber, los_pe-ces en el rí-o, por ver a Dios na-cer.
drink-ing yet once more, oh_ see them ce-le bra-ting, that Je-sus Christ is born.

Ya vienen los Reyes

Ya vie-nen los Re-yes,__ por los a-re-na-les,__ ya le traen al
The Three Wise Kings are com-ing,_ across the san-dy des-erts._ Among the gifts they're

Ni-ño__ muy ri-cos pa-ña-les. Man-za-ni-ta ver-de, ho-jas de li-
bring-ing,_ are the soft-est dia-pers. Oh lit-tle green ap-ples and le-mon tree

[1.] [2.]

món, la Vir-gen Ma-rí-a ma-dre del Se-ñor. Man-za-ni-ta ñor.
leaves, the sweet Vir-gin Ma-ry gives Ba-by a kiss. Oh lit-tle green kiss.